High-Tech
DIY Projects
with
Musical
Instruments

Maggie Murphy

PowerKiDS
press

New York

Published in 2015 by The Rosen Publishing Group, Inc.
29 East 21st Street, New York, NY 10010

First Edition

Editors: Jennifer Way and Jacob Seifert
Book Design: Andrew Povolny
Photo Research: Katie Stryker

Photo Credits: Cover Greg Tucker; p. 4 Gallo Images/Vetta/Getty Images; p. 5 veroxdale/Shutterstock.com; p. 6 Mac Miller/Hemera/Getty Images; p. 7 James Woodson/Photodisc/Getty Images; p. 8 AFP/DDP /Getty Images; p. 9 Olaf Diegel; p. 10 Stocktrek Images/Getty Images; p. 11 Martin Diebel/Getty Images; p. 12 RuprechJudit/iStock/Thinkstock; p. 13 sumatept/iStock/Thinkstock; p. 14 Dave King/Dorling Kindersley /Getty Images; p. 15 Fuse/Thinkstock; p. 17 Zero Creatives/Image Source/Getty Images; pp. 18–19, 24–25 Katie Stryker; p. 20 Image Source White/Thinkstock; p. 21 WimL/Shutterstock.com; p. 22 RTimages/iStock/ Thinkstock; p. 23 John Howard/Photodisc/Getty Images; pp. 26–27 Alexander Nicholson/Photonica/Getty Images; p. 28 c.d. stone; p. 29 Mark Hannaford/AWL Hannaford/Getty Images.

Library of Congress Cataloging-in-Publication Data

Murphy, Maggie.
 High-tech DIY projects with musical instruments / by Maggie Murphy. — First edition.
     pages cm. — (Maker kids)
 Includes index.
 ISBN 978-1-4777-6674-3 (library binding) — ISBN 978-1-4777-6680-4 (pbk.) —
ISBN 978-1-4777-6661-3 (6-pack)
 1. Musical instruments—Construction—Juvenile literature. I. Title.
 ML460.M942 2015
 784.192'3—dc23
                        2014004733

Manufactured in the United States of America

CPSIA Compliance Information: Batch #WS14PK9: For Further Information contact Rosen Publishing, New York, New York at 1-800-237-9932

Contents

Musical Instruments

It is fun and easy to make your own musical instruments. In fact, when you make a musical instrument, you get to have fun over and over! It's fun to make the instrument and it's even more fun to play it.

These drums from West Africa are called *djembes*. They are often made by hand.

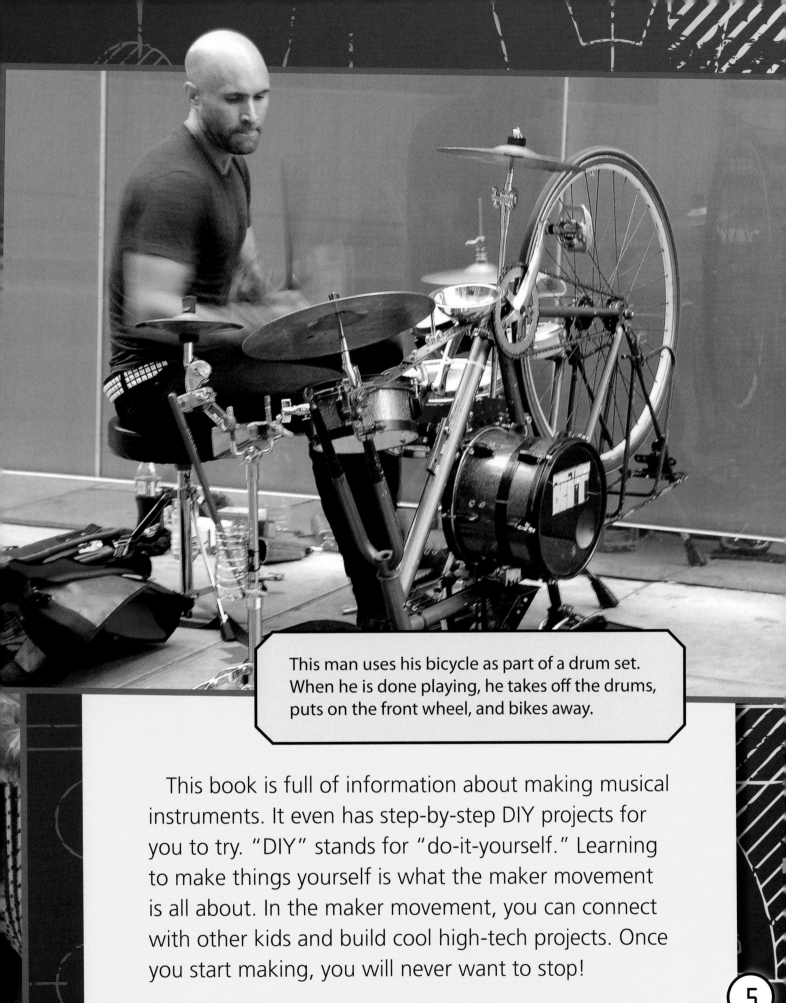

This man uses his bicycle as part of a drum set. When he is done playing, he takes off the drums, puts on the front wheel, and bikes away.

This book is full of information about making musical instruments. It even has step-by-step DIY projects for you to try. "DIY" stands for "do-it-yourself." Learning to make things yourself is what the maker movement is all about. In the maker movement, you can connect with other kids and build cool high-tech projects. Once you start making, you will never want to stop!

Instruments in Groups

Most instruments can be put into one of the four instrument families, or groups. Which family an instrument belongs in depends on how it makes sound.

The string family has instruments that make sound with strings. The acoustic guitar and cello are stringed instruments. Woodwinds make sound when you blow into them. They are very straight with few, if any, curves. Woodwinds include the flute, clarinet, and recorder.

The bassoon is a woodwind instrument. The player blows into the reed, the piece at the end of the tube. The vibration of the reed helps the bassoon make sound.

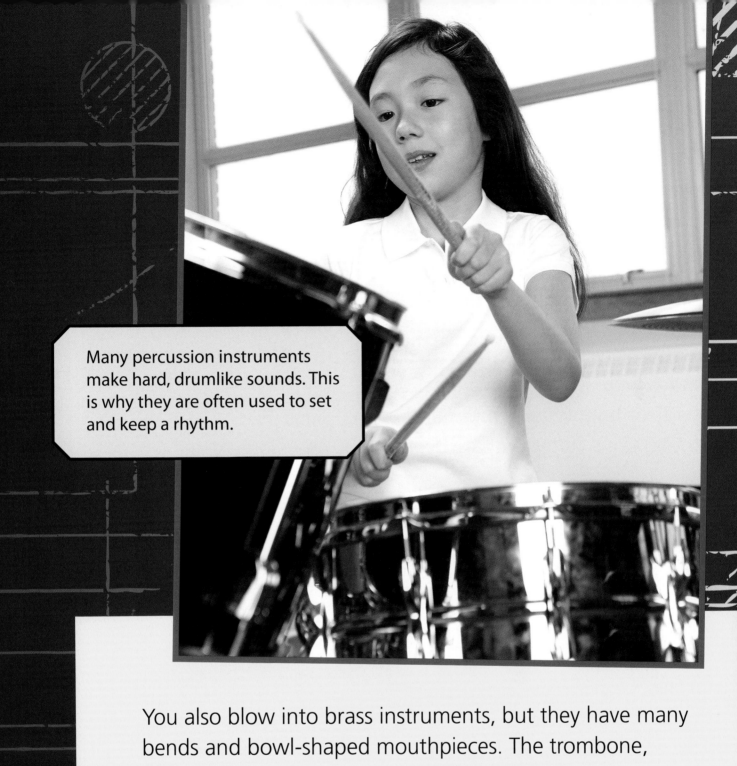

Many percussion instruments make hard, drumlike sounds. This is why they are often used to set and keep a rhythm.

You also blow into brass instruments, but they have many bends and bowl-shaped mouthpieces. The trombone, trumpet, and tuba are brass instruments. Percussion instruments make sound when you shake or hit them. These include drums, cymbals, and the tambourine.

Another type of instrument is electronic. Some, such as keyboards, make electronic sounds. Other electronic instruments, such as electric guitars, make sound that is **amplified**, or made louder, electronically.

Musical Materials

Early humans made music by singing, clapping, and stomping. They also banged rocks and sticks against things. These were the earliest percussion instruments. Ancient flutes were made from animal bones. Drums were built from parts of **hollow** tree trunks and animal skins. Scientists have found bone flutes that are over 42,000 years old.

Ancient instruments, like this bone flute, help scientists learn more about how long humans have been playing music.

3D printers are machines that make objects by putting layers of melted material on top of each other. The body of this electric guitar was made with a 3D printer.

Recycling for Music

Musical instruments can be very expensive. However, throughout history, people have made their own instruments very cheaply with recycled materials. For example, steel drums are made from the bottoms of large steel barrels. These instruments were invented on the Caribbean island of Trinidad in the 1940s.

Today, there are hundreds of commonly used musical instruments. Modern instruments are made from wood, metal, plastic, and **fiberglass**. One of the newest technologies used to make musical instruments is **3D printing**.

Some people even experiment with building their own instruments using household items, craft materials, and things found at hardware stores. You can, too!

What Is Sound?

When something **vibrates**, it moves back and forth very quickly, moving the air around it. That air bumps into and moves even more air. This happens over and over again, making waves of air that move away from the thing that is vibrating. When those waves reach your ears, you hear sound.

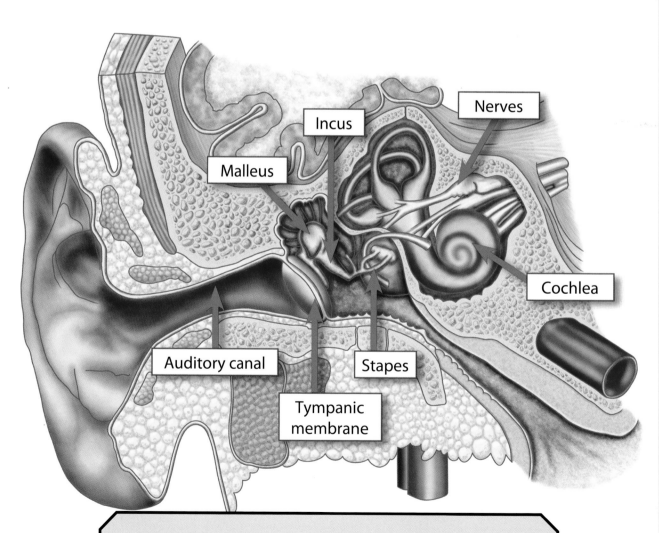

Nerves

Incus

Malleus

Cochlea

Auditory canal

Stapes

Tympanic membrane

Different parts in your ears work together to change vibrations into sounds that your brain can recognize.

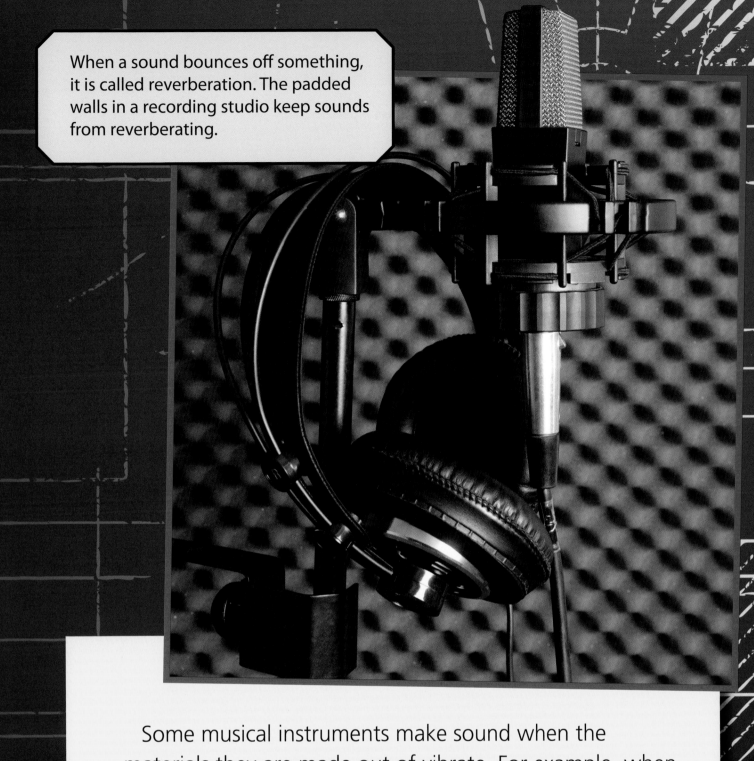

When a sound bounces off something, it is called reverberation. The padded walls in a recording studio keep sounds from reverberating.

Some musical instruments make sound when the materials they are made out of vibrate. For example, when you strum or pluck a string on a guitar, the string vibrates to make sound. When you hit or shake a percussion instrument, such as a drum, the surface vibrates.

Some instruments make sound when the air inside of them vibrates. This is why a flute makes sound when you blow into it.

The different sounds musical instruments make are called notes. The reason why notes sound different can be explained by **frequency** and **pitch**. The faster something vibrates, the more waves it makes in the air and the higher pitched it will sound. The slower it vibrates, the fewer the waves it makes in the air and the deeper it will sound. Frequency is how many waves a vibrating object makes in 1 second. Pitch is how high or low a noise sounds.

Sheet music tells musicians which notes to play. Each line and space matches a musical note, or pitch.

A musician can play many notes by pressing the keys, or buttons, on an instrument. This changes the instrument's shape and sound.

Some instruments can play only one note. Others are designed to play many notes. To play different notes, a musician has to change the size of an instrument's vibrating parts. For example, when a guitar player presses on a string, the part of the string that vibrates gets shorter.

Timbre

Two different types of instruments can play the same note at the same volume for the same length of time, but those notes will sound different. This aspect of music is called timbre, or color. This explains why a guitar sounds different from a piano.

Creative Spaces for Makers

Doing DIY projects by yourself is fun! However, you can learn a lot by **collaborating**, or working, with others. There might be a place in your **community** where you can meet other kids, borrow tools, and work on awesome projects. These creative community centers may be called maker spaces, hacker spaces, or DIY clubs. Check the list found at Makezine.com/maker-community -groups to see if there is one near you.

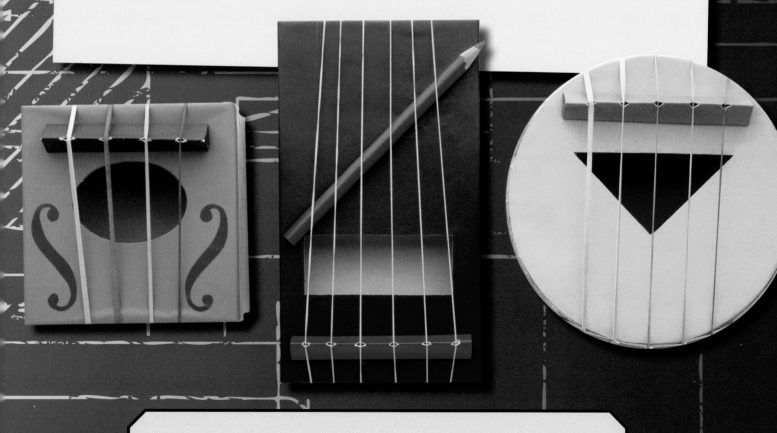

A group working together can make multiple instruments that sound good when played together.

If your parents have tools at your house, ask them to help you make an instrument!

If there are no creative community spaces nearby, ask your guardian, teacher, or librarian about starting one. Schools and libraries are great places to start maker spaces! Read more about starting your own maker space at Makerspace.com.

Simple Percussion Instruments

Percussion instruments are some of the quickest instruments to make. This is because you can turn almost anything into a percussion instrument by hitting, shaking, or scraping it.

Percussion instruments can be pitched or unpitched. A pitched percussion instrument is made or tuned so that it will play specific notes. Many percussion instruments are unpitched, meaning that they do not produce specific musical notes.

A shaker is one of the easiest unpitched instruments to make. You just need to find something that is hollow and put some small objects into it. When you shake the instrument, the small pieces inside of it bounce around, causing vibrations in the material that makes up the hollow object. Turn the page to learn more about making shakers.

Metal pots and pans make great percussion instruments. Bang on a few and see if you can tell the difference in the sounds they make.

Mini Project: Simple Shaker

You will need:

- 2 small plastic or paper cups
- Uncooked rice or dried beans
- Hot-glue gun
- Art supplies

There are many ways to make a simple shaker. This project shows you just one way you can do this. Make sure to have an adult help you use the hot-glue gun so you don't hurt yourself.

1) Fill one cup about two-thirds of the way up with uncooked rice or dried beans.

2) Have an adult help you squeeze hot glue onto the rim of the cup.

Shakers will sound different if they have rice, corn, or beans inside of them. Make a few different kinds and see if you can hear the difference.

3) Place the second cup upside down on top of the first cup. Press down so that the rims of the cups seal together.

4) Decorate the cups. You can draw on them, glue paper or ribbons onto them, or do anything you like! Once you like how it looks, your shaker is ready to play!

Make a Diddley Bow

Once you have made a simple shaker, you might want to try making a more **complex** musical instrument. A diddley bow is a great place to start!

In the past, if a child practiced enough with his diddley bow, he was given a guitar, which has more strings and is harder to play.

Slides are tubes that fit over your finger. You can also use a glass bottle or jar as a slide to play your diddley bow.

Diddley bows are one-string guitars. They sit on your lap and are played slide style. Slide-style instruments are played with both hands. With one hand, you press and slide an object called a slide up and down the string to change the notes. With the other hand, you tap or pluck the string.

The diddley bow may be a simple instrument, but it has played a big part in American culture. It has been used by countless kids and influenced the blues. Diddley bows were often given to kids as a first instrument. Diddley bows are also called jitterbugs or one-strings.

You will need an adult's help for this project. It involves wiring, which can be dangerous if it is done incorrectly. You will also need to wear safety goggles because the glass jar or bottle you are using could break. Safety is the most important part of any DIY project.

You will need:

- 1 30-inch (76 cm) wooden board
- 1 guitar string
- 1 clean, thick glass jar with straight walls or glass bottle
- 1 guitar pickup, with mounting screws
- 1 concave guitar jack and plate, with mounting screws
- 1 guitar cable
- 1 eye screw
- 3 nails
- 1 guitar amp
- Screwdriver
- Pair of pliers
- Hammer
- Wire strippers
- Electrical tape
- Safety goggles
- Work gloves

If you use a jar for your diddley bow, the walls must be thick. They must also be straight up and down. Many jam jars are good for this project.

Once you have all of things you need and an adult to help you, turn the page and get started!

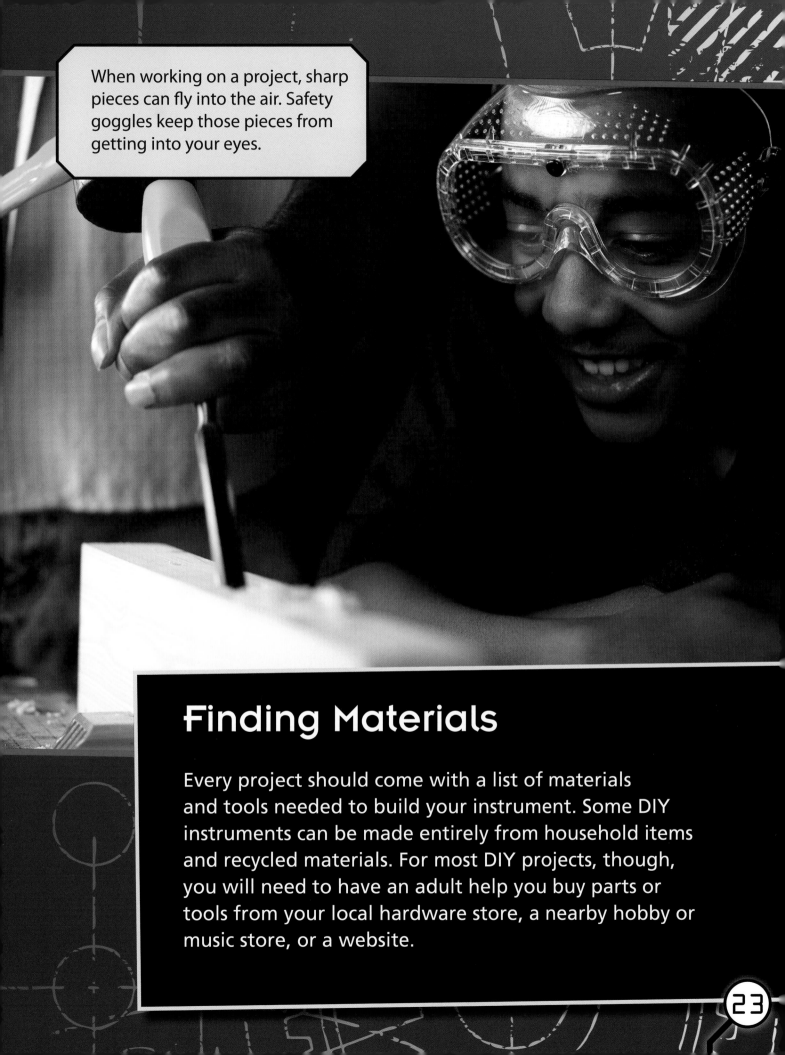

When working on a project, sharp pieces can fly into the air. Safety goggles keep those pieces from getting into your eyes.

Finding Materials

Every project should come with a list of materials and tools needed to build your instrument. Some DIY instruments can be made entirely from household items and recycled materials. For most DIY projects, though, you will need to have an adult help you buy parts or tools from your local hardware store, a nearby hobby or music store, or a website.

Build It Step-by-Step

1

Center the guitar pickup on the board 8 to 10 inches (20–25 cm) from one end. Screw it in.

2

Center an eye screw 1 to 2 inches (2–5 cm) from the end of the board that is closest to the pickup. Screw it in.

3

Center a nail 1 to 2 inches (2–5 cm) on the end of the board farthest from the pickup. Angle it away from the pickup. Nail it in just enough so that it is firmly in place.

4

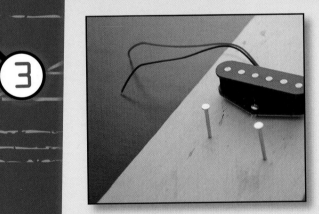

Nail in two nails about 3 inches (8 cm) from the pickup on the side closer to the eye screw.

5

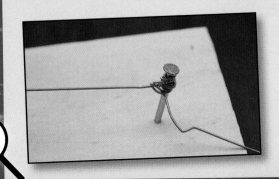

Loop the guitar string through the eye screw and then through the eyelet on the string. Run the string down the board, but do not pull it very tight. Loop it around the nail several times. Make a tight knot.

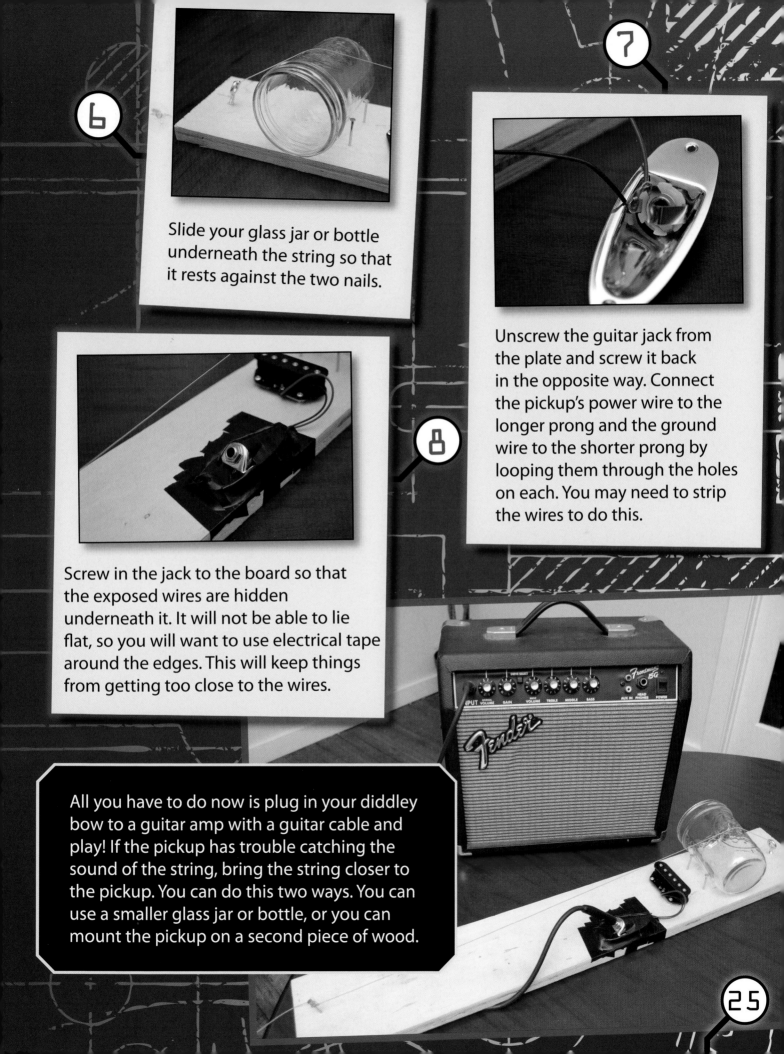

6

Slide your glass jar or bottle underneath the string so that it rests against the two nails.

7

Unscrew the guitar jack from the plate and screw it back in the opposite way. Connect the pickup's power wire to the longer prong and the ground wire to the shorter prong by looping them through the holes on each. You may need to strip the wires to do this.

8

Screw in the jack to the board so that the exposed wires are hidden underneath it. It will not be able to lie flat, so you will want to use electrical tape around the edges. This will keep things from getting too close to the wires.

All you have to do now is plug in your diddley bow to a guitar amp with a guitar cable and play! If the pickup has trouble catching the sound of the string, bring the string closer to the pickup. You can do this two ways. You can use a smaller glass jar or bottle, or you can mount the pickup on a second piece of wood.

Try These Projects!

The Internet is a great place to look for projects with step-by-step instructions and video **tutorials**, or lessons. The next paragraphs describe some fun projects. Links to each of them can be found in the Projects Links box at the end of this chapter.

How you set up an instrument can have a big effect on how it is played. This homemade stand arranges metal bowls and pots into a set of drums.

An instrument that is quick to make and easy to carry around with you is a thumb piano. You can even alter the design to add more keys.

Instructables.com is a website with hundreds of DIY projects for you to make. One of them teaches you how to make a flute from a PVC pipe. Another project uses an Arduino™ board to create a high-tech digital xylophone.

Projects Links

Thumb Piano - Popularmechanics.com/home/how-to-plans/woodworkin /step-by-step-guides-offbeat-diy-projects-3
PVC Flute - Instructables.com/id/Making-Simple-PVC-Flutes
Arduino Xylophone - Instructables.com/id/Arduino-Xylophone

Keep Experimenting!

Buying a musical instrument can be expensive, but now you know how to make your own! If you take what you have learned about sound, you can even try designing your own instrument from scratch. Try using household items, recycled materials, 3D-printed parts, or high-tech electronics kits!

3D-Printed Thumb Piano

Another fun way to create musical instruments is by using a 3D printer. One unique instrument you can make is a thumb piano. All you have to do is download the free ready-made file from Repables.com/r/255 and use a 3D printer to print it. If you're not familiar with 3D printing, read another book in the Maker Kids series, *High-Tech DIY Projects with 3D Printers*. It has everything you need to know to get started making your own 3D-printed instruments and more.

Kids all around the world are making their own musical instruments, like this guitar. A well-made instrument can give you a lifetime of music.

Building musical instruments is also a great way to get involved with the maker movement. In the maker movement, you can meet other kids, share your ideas, and learn more about science and technology. Once you have basic projects down, there are endless high-tech DIY projects to try.

More About Making

The lists below show you more ways to learn about making musical instruments. You can also ask an adult to help you use the library and search the Internet for other projects, books, and places to buy supplies!

Books

Niven, Felicia Lowenstein. *Nifty Thrifty Music Crafts*. Berkeley Heights, NJ. Enslow Elementary, 2007.

Orr, Mike. *Handmade Music Factory*. East Petersburg, PA. Fox Chapel Publishing, 2011.

Websites

• Instructables.com has new DIY projects uploaded every day.
• Make instruments, earn a badge, and have fun at Diy.org/skills/instrumentmaker.
• Find Arduino™ music projects at Makershed.com/Music_Audio _Projects_s/128.htm.
• Find ideas for making 3D-printed instruments at 3d-printing.net /tags/musical-instruments.

Glossary

amplified (AM-pluh-fyd) Made louder.

collaborating (kuh-LA-buh-ray-ting) More than one person working toward a common goal.

community (kuh-MYOO-nih-tee) A place where people live and work together.

complex (kom-PLEKS) Not simple.

fiberglass (FY-ber-glas) A material made of glass and other things.

frequency (FREE-kwen-see) The number of waves a vibrating object makes in 1 second.

hollow (HOL-oh) Having a hole through the center.

pitch (PICH) How high or low a sound is.

3D printing (THREE-DEE-PRIN-ting) A process in which thin layers of soft material are squeezed on top of each other to create a three-dimensional object.

tutorials (too-TAWR-ee-ulz) Lessons.

vibrates (VY-brayts) Moves back and forth quickly.

Index

A
air, 10–12

C
cello, 6
clarinet, 6
community, 14
curves, 6

D
drum(s), 7–9, 11

F
fiberglass, 9
flute(s), 6, 8, 11, 27
frequency, 12

G
guitar(s), 6–7, 11,
    13, 21

M
maker movement, 5, 29
mouthpieces, 7

P
pitch, 12

R
recorder, 6

S
shaker(s), 16, 18–20

sound(s), 6–7,
    10–12, 25, 28
string(s), 6,
    11, 13, 21–22,
    24–25

T
3D printing,
    9, 28
trombone, 7
trumpet, 7
tuba, 7
tutorials, 26

W
woodwinds, 6

Websites

Due to the changing nature of Internet links, PowerKids Press has developed an online list of websites related to the subject of this book. This site is updated regularly. Please use this link to access the list:
www.powerkidslinks.com/maker/music/